A CLOISTERS BESTIARY

the metropolitan museum of art

a cloisters bestiary

PREPARED BY

RICHARD h. RANDALL, JR.

NEW YORK, N.Y. 1960

Most of the reproductions are from photographs taken
especially for this publication by William F. Pons.
Those of the sculptured lion (page 5), the tigers
(page 29), and the Harpy (page 37) are by F. L. Kenett.

FRONTISPIECE: The Unicorn in Captivity (slightly cropped). *French or Flemish Tapestry, about 1500. Gift of John D. Rockefeller, Jr., 1937.*

First printing 1960, 5000 copies.
Second printing 1965, 6000 copies.

Library of Congress Catalog Card No. 60-12054
©The Metropolitan Museum of Art, New York, 1960

Ꭺ ᏴᎬᏚᎢᏆᎪᎡᎽ, as the name so plainly suggests, is a book about beasts. It is a form of natural history that was widely read and respected in the Middle Ages. Although it was intended as a serious and factual commentary on the animal kingdom, the medieval bestiary presented an enchanting mixture of fact and fancy, often enlivened by illustrations that spurred the imagination to its own devices. To this were added interpretations of natural phenomena that served as moral and religious lessons to the reader.

The medieval bestiary appeared in many versions, and none can be ascribed to a single author. Much of the information in all the variant forms was derived from the *Physiologus*, an anonymous book which, early in the Christian Era, summarized and codified what the ancients had known or believed to be true about the animals, birds, and reptiles of the earth. In the *Physiologus* are echoes of Herodotus's observations on the natural world, and the *Historia Animalium* of Aristotle as well as the works of Pliny the Elder, Solinus, Aelian, and other Roman naturalists are drawn upon. Saint Ambrose in the fourth century and Saint Isidore of Seville in the sixth enlarged upon the *Physiologus* and defined its religious messages with parallels found in texts from the Bible and the Septuagint.

Each scribe who brought forth a fresh copy of the popular bestiary undoubtedly added to his version information based on further hearsay or upon his personal experience. He would have suppressed anything he considered fallacious. Since most of the material was taken on faith from earlier authorities, and since some good part of it concerned phenomena that could only be observed beyond the horizon of the medieval European world, it is not strange that the unicorn and other fabulous beasts were accepted as real. The contemporary reader had no reasonable way to distinguish fact from fancy in the stories that reached him from the world beyond his own certain knowledge. A unicorn, after all, is quite as likely as a whale or an elephant. It is certainly a more reasonable creature than the rhinoceros with which its story is partly confused.

What might seem more credulous in the medieval writer are his interpretations of phenomena he correctly observed. He accurately notes that birds lose their feathers and that snakes shed their skins, but in his love of symbolism he equates these natural developments with doting parenthood and with rejuvenation. Other observations, such as the migration of birds and the existence of two-headed reptiles, were denied as spurious by eighteenth-century naturalists, only to be proved true in our own time. Animals have always fascinated mankind, and the idea of the bestiary has never died. Modern writers and artists, notably Toulouse-Lautrec and Saul Steinberg, have continued to provide fresh interpretations of the world of beasts.

This present bestiary approximates such texts as appeared in medieval copies that have come down to us and relates them to the figures of animals from the Middle Ages that may be seen at The Cloisters. The religious morals and parallels have been largely omitted as of limited interest to the modern reader, and to keep the text within modest bounds. A few have been retained to suggest the nature of such interpretations. The text is based largely on the translations by T. H. White of a Cambridge University Library manuscript (II.24.6) in his *Book of Beasts*. Excerpts have been added from Bishop Theobald's *Metrical Bestiary* of the thirteenth century and from other early bestiaries including Bodleian Manuscript 601 and Morgan Library Manuscript 81.

In a few cases the figures here illustrated are not exact counterparts of the beasts described in the texts, a confusion not uncommon in the original manuscripts. For instance, the siren in the Cambridge bestiary is described as a Harpy but is illustrated as a mermaid. In our book a heron serves to illustrate the text of the crane. However, for the most part our beasts have been correctly described. Occasionally, in a spirit of pure fun, they are depicted in a comic manner, as in the case of the goat, pursued by a weasel-like creature, who bows a rake over a jawbone as though he were playing a stringed instrument. It is hoped that the *Cloisters Bestiary* will help the reader to appreciate better the variety of fascinating animals that abound in medieval art.

THE STORY of the creation of the fishes, and fowls, and animals is told most truly in the Book of Genesis.

And God created great whales, and every living creature that moveth, which the waters brought forth abundantly, after their kind, and every winged fowl after his kind: and God saw that it was good.

And God blessed them saying, be fruitful and multiply, and fill the waters in the seas, and let fowl multiply in the earth....

And God said, Let the earth bring forth the living creature after his kind, cattle and creeping thing, and beast of the earth after his kind: and it was so.

Detail of an altarpiece · *Spanish (Castille), late XIV century · Purchase, 1925*

the LION is the king of beasts. Like a king, he takes only one wife. He is a mighty beast and you can tell his nature from the curl of his mane. A lion with a short curly mane is peaceful, while one with straight hair is ferocious. He is known for his terrible roaring voice, which often frightens other animals so that they freeze in their tracks and cannot run away. Although he has much courage, a lion fears the creaking of wheels and burning fire.

There are three main things to remember about the lion. First, he has a beautiful tufted tail, and when he goes for walks up tall mountains, which is his wont, he is sometimes spied and pursued by hunters. The lion then uses his tail to erase his own tracks from the ground, so that the hunters lose his spoor and cannot follow him.

Secondly, the lion is ever on guard, for he sleeps with his eyes open.

Thirdly, the lioness bears her cubs dead. She mourns over them for three days; then the lion comes and breathes life into them. This is a parallel to the death of Jesus, for on the third day the Father Almighty came and raised him from the dead.

The lion does not get angry unless he is wounded and he kills only men for food, rather than women or children. He is kind to captives and allows them to return

4

home and he spares those who have fallen. He eats only on alternate days. Being careful of overeating, when he has had too much, he puts his paw into his mouth and removes the extra meat. He will not eat from a former kill, for he dislikes leftover food.

When the lion is sick, he searches the forest for a monkey which he eats to be cured. He fears a cock, especially a white one, and the sting of the scorpion and the snake can kill him, though he can crush them with his paws.

Fresco from San Pedro de Arlanza · *Spanish, about 1220* · *Purchase, 1931*

Relief from San Leonardo, Zamora · *Spanish, mid-XIII century*
Joseph Pulitzer Fund, 1916

BEARS are curious creatures with thick and wonderfully furry coats. They are strong in their bodies and paws, but their heads are small and weak. Often they stand upright like a man.

The she-bear brings forth cubs in only thirty days without any shape or feature at all. She has, however, an infinitely clever tongue and with this she licks her shapeless offspring into proper bear-shape. At this task she spends fourteen days. She is then so exhausted that she falls asleep in such a stupor that nothing, not even the horns or spears of the hunters, can wake her, and she sleeps for three months.

A sick bear that has eaten the poisonous fruits of the mandrake knows that it can cure itself by eating ants. It also heals its sores with the plant mullein. Of all the food in the world, however, the bear prefers honey. It will spend hours in the forest seeking the hives of bees with their succulent combs.

In the winter bears are wont to go into their caves to sleep and lust. There they prepare for themselves fine private apartments by erecting earthen dividing walls.

Capital from the Trie Cloister • *French (Bigorre), late XV century • Purchase, 1925*

Enlarged detail from the cover of an engraved silver beaker.
German (Ingolstadt), about 1460 • Purchase, 1950

the wolf

is a cunning and dangerous beast, well known for his greediness. When he is hungry he slyly goes to the sheepfold at night and lies down like a tame dog with the sheep. In his cleverness, he goes against the wind so the sheep dogs will not notice him and if, by chance, the wolf steps on a twig or makes any noise with his paw, he bites the paw and chastises it for betraying him.

The wolf is made with a stiff neck and can never turn his head to look backwards. He has great wicked teeth and much strength in his chest and paws, while his hind parts are small and weak. It is said that on the wolf's back is a tuft of aphrodisiac hair, which is effective only if taken from a live wolf. The she-wolf whelps but once a year and then always in May and in the thunder. She is very crafty in finding food for her cubs and always hunts far away from her cave, rather than near it.

At night the awesome eyes of the wolf shine like lamps. If the wolf sees a man before it has been seen, it strikes him dumb with its eyes and may then conquer him easily. If the wolf is seen first, however, it has great fear and loses its power to run away.

Detail from the Unicorn Tapestries · *French or Flemish, about 1500* · *Gift of John D. Rockefeller, Jr., 1937*

8

the panther is a beautiful animal with a tawny coat spotted with black. It is not only handsome but very kind. Among the animals it counts only the dragon its enemy.

After the panther has eaten its dinner, it retires to its cave and curls up for three days to sleep. When it awakes, a lovely ringing sound comes from its mouth, together with a delightful smell of blossoms and herbs, like allspice. When the animals of the forest have heard the noise, they come to the panther and follow it wherever it goes because of the fragrance of its breath. Only the dragon flees from the noise. He fears the panther, and retreats to his cave to avoid the panther's hated breath.

The mother panther has cubs only once in her life; then she has three. The reason for this is clear, for baby panthers have sharp claws and, being impatient to be born, they scratch and scar the inside of the mother. When they are born the mother is so injured that she can never again have cubs. So it is with many animals with sharp claws.

Detail from the Unicorn Tapestries · *French or Flemish, about 1500* · *Gift of John D. Rockefeller, Jr., 1937*

9

the elephant is biggest of all the beasts. He is as big as a

mountain. He is an odd-looking creature with a very long nose, like a snake, which is called a trunk. With this he eats all the leaves off his favorite bushes. For his defence he has not only his huge size and weight, for he can crush enemies beneath his feet, but also a pair of ivory tusks. It is because of his size and strength that the Indians and Persians build wooden towers on his back from which to fight one another with javelins.

The elephant is the most chaste of animals and must find a rare plant, the mandrake, in order to conceive. Having done so, the female elephant carries the baby for two years before it is born. At the time of the birth, she greatly fears her enemy, the dragon, and while the male elephant guards her on the bank, she goes into the river and delivers the baby. Elephants only conceive once in their lives and then they bring forth only one baby. This is strange as they live to be three hundred years old.

The elephant is so constructed that he has no joints in his knees, which makes it impossible for him to rise if he falls. Because of this he sleeps leaning against the bole of a large tree that will sustain his weight. In order to catch the elephant, the hunter saws the tree halfway through. When the elephant comes to sleep he falls with the tree to the ground. If other elephants hear the fallen one trumpeting for help, they come and try to raise him, but without success. Finally a small elephant comes and lifts up the fallen one, in the same way that Christ in lowly human form came to save man from the Devil and raise him up again.

10

The elephant is faithful to his wife and is by nature very gentle. If a man is lost in the forests, he will lead him back to the paths of the world. Because he likes the companionship of his fellows the elephant travels in herds. If one is angered, however, he can become fierce and pull up great trees with his trunk and crush buildings beneath his feet. He fears the unicorn, who can wound him in the belly, and even more so, the tiny mouse.

Lid of a Minnekästchen · *German or Swiss, XV century* · *Purchase, 1955*

Enlarged detail from The Hours of Jeanne d'Évreux · *French (Paris), 1325-28* *Purchase, 1954*

the ᎴᎾᏩ is the wisest animal and the one that enjoys man's company the most. He can learn his own name, will come when called, and will greatly respect the man who trains and feeds him.

Dogs are found in many varieties. Some have fine noses to hunt the beasts of the forest and fangs to rend them; others are gentle and guard the sheep from the wolf. Those that defend the hearths of their masters will set on any intruder or thief and protect the home to the death if necessary. They accompany men on all their errands and will even guard their bodies in death.

It is told that when King Garamantes was captured in battle, two hundred of his hounds banded together and rescued him from his enemies. The hound of Jason refused food after the death of his master and died mourning; while that of King Lisimachus jumped onto the funeral pyre of the king and was consumed with him. One account tells of a dog in Rome that accompanied its master to prison and howled piteously when he was executed. The citizens of Rome tried to comfort him with food, but he took it to the body of his master. When the corpse was finally thrown into the Tiber, the hound jumped in the water and kept the body from sinking.

It is also well known that dogs can often find the culprit of a crime. One man was walking in Antioch at dusk with his dog, when he was slain by an unfaithful servant. The dog stood by the body until a crowd had gathered. Thinking that this would throw off suspicion, the murderer joined the crowd. With a howl and a leap the dog fastened on him. Such was the obviousness of this testimony that the servant could not conceal his guilt.

The dog is of a temperate and balanced nature. He uses his reason to find the correct answer. When a dog is tracking a rabbit, for instance, he is seldom fooled by false trails and will try each scent with his nose until he can select the right path. The dog furthermore knows how to heal its own wounds by licking them with its tongue. The tongue of a puppy makes a salve to heal the sicknesses of men.

A dog can, however, be fooled. If he has a fine piece of meat in his mouth and sees its reflection in the water, a dog will jump to seize the meat in the reflection and thus lose the one he carried in his mouth.

Detail from the Unicorn Tapestries • *French or Flemish, about 1500* • *Gift of John D. Rockefeller, Jr., 1937*

Detail from the Tomb of Don Alvaro de Cabrera • *Spanish (Urgel), 1299-1314* • *Purchase, 1948*

the weasel

reminds one of an elongated mouse. It lives by stealth and hunts mostly snakes and mice. Some weasels live among men in their very houses. These are clever and when they have new babies lie every night with them in a different lair. Some say that weasels conceive through the ear and give birth through the mouth; others put it the other way around, that they conceive through the mouth and give birth by ear.

NOTE: The story of the weasel, or ichneumon, was applied to all members of the family including the stoat, the ferret, and the ermine as illustrated.

Detail from the Unicorn Tapestries · *French or Flemish, about 1500* · *Gift of John D. Rockefeller, Jr., 1937*

14

Capital from Saint-Michel de Cuxa · *French (Languedoc), second half of the XII century · Purchase, 1925*

the monkey is named Simia in Latin because it is so similar to man. These creatures also have the ability to reason like men. They have knowledge of the sky and when the moon is new they are exceedingly joyful. At the full moon, and even at the half moon, they become depressed. The monkey is an ugly animal to look at for he has wide, squashed nostrils. He has no tail.

Monkeys are excellent at imitating men, and hunters are said to take advantage of this to catch them. A clever hunter will leave a pair of boots beneath the monkey's tree, and the monkey cannot resist the temptation of pulling them on. The hunter quickly returns and captures the monkey, who too late finds that he cannot climb a tree wearing boots.

It is in the nature of the mother monkey that if she has twins, she will adore one of them and hate the other. The one she adores she carries in her arms and fondles, while the one she hates must ride on her back, holding on with its own arms. It often happens that hunters come to find the monkey and chase the

15

mother with her twins. To escape, the mother seeks refuge in the top of a tree, and as she climbs she must drop the baby she loves on the ground. The one she hates, however, still clings to her back and is consequently saved.

Certain varieties of monkeys, like cynocephali, or baboons, are fierce animals, always biting one another and leaping wildly about. They live mostly in Ethiopia. Sphinxes are monkeys, too, but are much tamer and can become pets.

Enlarged detail of an enameled beaker (Monkey Cup) · *Flemish, about 1460 · Purchase, 1952*

16

the wild boar is a fierce and savage animal that has no fear
of death. He has two cruel tusks in his mouth with which he rends his enemies.
When the tusks get dull, he whets them on the trunks of trees or seeks out the
plant marjoram, which cleanses and sharpens his fangs. Bartholomeus Anglicus
tells us that the boar has a natural shield of hard flesh on his right side. When
he is attacked, he opposes that to the spear of the hunter. Even after he is pierced
with the arrow or spear, he will turn and seek to tear his enemy apart with his
cruel tusks. In real fury he whets his tusks and foams at the mouth and is a terrible
sight to see.

Coats of arms from St. Guilhem-le-Desert · *French (Hérault), early XIV century*
Purchase, 1925

the goat

is fond of scaling the highest and rockiest mountain peaks. From his high perches he can see far away with his sharp eyes and can discern the hunter from the wayfarer. In the same way Christ perceived the wickedness of Judas from afar and said, "Behold, the man who shall betray me is approaching."

When the goat feeds on the mountain slope he wanders always higher and higher to find the herbs he loves. If he is wounded the goat, like the stag, runs to seek the herb dittany to cure his wounds.

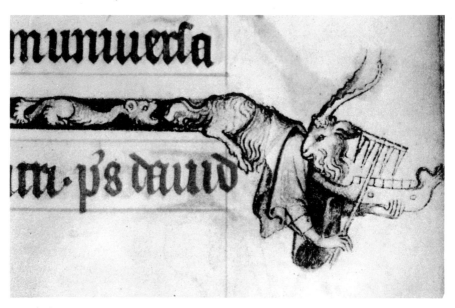

Enlarged detail from The Hours of Jeanne d'Évreux · *French (Paris), 1325-28 Purchase, 1954*

the antelope

is so fleet of foot that he cannot be caught by hunters. He has great horns with many prongs, like a saw blade, and can, if he chooses, cut down great forest trees. When the antelope is thirsty, he goes to quench his thirst in the great river Euphrates. There on the banks grows a plant

with long, wavy twigs called Herecine. As the antelope drinks, he likes to fence with the wavy arms of the Herecine and his horns often become entangled. He then bellows aloud in his plight and the hunter, who waits to hear the cry, comes swiftly and kills the beast.

Detail of a lusterware dish · *Spanish (Valencia), 1420-30 · Purchase, 1956*

19

the ox is a kind animal. He so misses his companion at the yoke, if he be absent, that the one will call for the other the whole day long. Oxen are helpful to man in pulling the plow. They can be taught to pull evenly and will thresh the wheat and tread the flour. The ox-herd often pleases his oxen by whistling or singing a tune, which they readily enjoy.

The ox is sensitive to weather and desires to stay in the barn when it is going to rain. However, if the weather is going to change for the better, he looks out from the stable at the sky and the farmer knows that he wishes to work in the sunshine.

Some wild oxen in Germany have great horns on their heads. These are much favored for drinking horns at royal banquets for they have a great capacity.

Stained-glass roundel · *English, XV century* · *Purchase, 1932*

the squirrel is a tiny animal that is very easily angered. It is said that because of their nature squirrels often die of blind rage. They usually feast on the nuts of the forest, carefully biting the ends off the shells.

The squirrel is very sagacious about crossing a river or even an ocean. When he comes to the edge of the water he seeks a large dry leaf, a nutshell, or a large mushroom and makes a boat out of it. He paddles with his forepaws and at the same time raises his tail high into the air as a sail. Thus he is whisked smartly along by the wind and soon comes to the other shore.

❖

Detail from the Unicorn Tapestries · *French or Flemish, about 1500* · *Gift of John D. Rockefeller, Jr., 1937*

the sheep is the gentlest among all the animals. It has no means of defending itself and is very placid by nature. It is covered with fine wool but though all sheep look alike, the lamb can tell its own mother from the rest of the flock, and she in turn can find her own lamb among hundreds of others.

When cold weather is felt in the air, the sheep gets frantically hungry and greedily devours all the pasturage in sight. It eats the grass even down to the roots, hoping to eat it all before the first frost.

The sheep has always been the favored of all animals for sacrifice. The Gentiles preferred those with two long teeth, and the baby lamb was favored, even more than bulls, on the altars of the ancients.

Carved wood panel from Jumièges • *French (Normandy), early XVI century*
Purchase 1950

CAMELS are of two types. One is the dromedary, which has a single hump on its back and is swifter. The other, bred in Arabia, has two humps, as do the camels of the Bactrians, which are the strongest. The hooves of the Bactrian camel are wide and padded so the creature can walk on the soft sands; they never wear away.

Camels are known for being able to overcome thirst. They drink but seldom and, when they do, they drink for the dryness of the past and of the future. They prefer muddy water to all other and will seek out a foul pool rather than a clean one. They live to be a hundred years old.

Most camels are of a nasty disposition. They hate horses foremost of all creatures. They are used to carry burdens over great distances. The smaller and swifter ones are used for riding. If the owner of a camel sells it, the camel mourns and grows ill, not for loss of his master, but because he thinks the price was too low.

Page from the Belles Heures of Jean, Duke of Berry · *French, 1410-13* · *Purchase, 1954*

horses

horses are animals of great spirit. They enjoy battles and are excited by the sound of trumpets and fighting. They suffer great anguish when they are conquered and exult in victory. In battle they recognize their enemies and often attack them with great kicking and biting. A horse knows his own master and will allow no other to ride on his back. It is even said that when the master dies the horse weeps for him. It is the only animal that approaches man in this.

The famous horse that bore Alexander the Great through many battles was called Bucephalus. Once this steed had been ridden by Alexander, he would never again allow any other upon his back. This was also true of the horse of Gaius Caesar. When the King of the Scythians was killed in battle, his horse bit and kicked to death his master's conqueror; and the horse of King Nicomedes would take no food after his master had been slain. When his horse was killed at the defeat of the Galatians, Antiochus jumped on that of the fallen Galatian general. The horse refused to obey the reins and plunged to the earth killing both himself and Antiochus.

Many horses live to be seventy years of age. The males generally have a longer life than the females. Their virility is removed by clipping their manes. It is said that a horse that dips his nostrils deep in the stream when drinking will prove a fine sire.

When a foal is born, it bears on its forehead a love charm of a tawny color, which is the shape and size of a dried fig. The mother licks this off with her tongue and hides it. If it is taken away she will not feed her colt. However, if this falls into the hands of a witch, it can be used to excite a man to love.

The ancients believed that four things were necessary in a fine horse: first, that he should be well formed and of goodly size, with a large chest and muscular limbs; secondly, that he should be beautiful, with a fine head, curved neck, and thick mane and tail; then, that he should show great spirit, which can be judged from the trembling of his limbs. Lastly, the horse should have a fine color. The ancients considered a chestnut horse the finest but others prefer the colors in this order: bay, golden, ruddy, chestnut, fawn, gray, roan, hoary, silver, white, flea-bitten, and black. Of all the colors, the worst is the piebald.

Horses fall into several types, the finest of which are spirited mounts that can carry ample weight in battle. Then there are work horses, which are large and fine for pulling but not for riding In between are the hackneys which may be used for all purposes as their masters see fit.

❊

Bronze aquamanile · *German,*
about 1400 · Purchase, 1947

Bronze aquamanile · *North European,*
XIV century · Purchase, 1947

the ass is a beast of burden which was domesticated long before the horse. It is very easy to catch an ass because it has no sense at all. If it is surrounded by men, it gets confused and surrenders. The ass is useful for work for it can carry a great load. It does not need attention, but rather fares better on complete neglect.

The wild ass is noted for recognizing the season of the Equinox. On the twenty-sixth day of March each year the ass brays twelve times in the day and twelve times in the night. People can mark the hours by its braying. Job suspected that the ass only brayed at other times when it was hungry, for he said, "Doth the wild ass bray when he hath grass?"

NOTE: The subject of the illustration refers to an ancient story in which an ass playing a lyre symbolizes foolishness.

Fresco from San Pedro de Arlanza • *Spanish, about 1220* • *Purchase, 1931*

26

the cat is a merry animal when it is young. It plays and leaps about and can be led to play with a straw. In older age it waxes fat and sleepy, but in spite of this, it is quick and fearsome to mice. When a cat with his stealth and cunning catches a mouse, he will play with him at his leisure. When the play is done he will eat the mouse. The cat is remarkable in one feature; if he is thrown down from a high place, he will land unharmed on his four feet. Also, his eyes shine so that he can see clearly in the dark.

In the season of love a cat will fight continually with other cats for his wife. There is great screeching and crying as they rend one another fiercely with their claws. The cat that has a fine pelt is proud of it and shows it off, but if his coat is damaged or burnt, he sits at home dejected. The cat with the fair coat must be quick or he may end up at the furrier's.

Enlarged details from The Hours of Jeanne d'Évreux • *French (Paris), 1325-28*
Purchase, 1954

the fox is a sly animal who always runs by a devious route to throw off pursuers. He often outwits the wily farmer who tries to protect his chickens, and steals them from him. Even more remarkable, the fox by his craft and cunning can deceive the sharp-eyed birds of the air. When he has found no suitable meal to eat, the fox daubs himself with red mud or something that resembles blood. Then he lies in an open place on his back with his tongue out, holding his breath. The crows and other birds seeing this, think that the fox is dead and they swoop down to feast on him. But he grabs the fattest of them and has a feast himself instead.

Enlarged detail from The Hours of Jeanne d'Évreux • *French (Paris), 1325-28*
Purchase, 1954

the TIGER is a beast of great speed, whose name derives from the Persian word for "arrow." The river Tigris was named for him because it is the swiftest river in the world. He can easily be recognized by the spots that cover his body. He lives principally in Hyrcania.

If a hunter chances upon the lair of the tiger and finds cubs there alone, he may steal one. When the tigress returns and discovers her loss, she races along the track of the hunter to save her cub. In spite of the speed of the hunter's horse, the tigress can soon overtake him. The hunter, in fear of his life, uses the following strategem to outwit the speedy carnivore: he throws a mirror down on the ground. Looking in it, the tigress thinks that her small reflection is her lost cub and she curls up around the mirror to suckle it. Thus the hunter escapes with his quarry. So out of the zealousness of motherhood the tigress loses her cub and her revenge.

Capital from San Martín, Fuentidueña · *Spanish (Segovia), late XII century* · *Loan from the Spanish Government*

29

The STAG is one of the noblest of beasts. He bears two horns proudly on his head. He is extremely fond of music and listens attentively with his ears standing up. When he puts his ears down, however, he cannot hear at all.

When a stag is ill or feels that he is getting old, he seeks the hole of a snake, his enemy. With his great nostrils he sucks forth the snake from his lair and devours him whole. The eating of the venomous serpent restores the stag's health. He then sheds his old skin and is young again. There is a plant called dittany which also is helpful to the stag, for when he has eaten it he is immune to the arrows of the hunters.

When they hear the hounds chasing them, stags run downwind so that their scent is carried away from the dogs. But often, if surprised, they stand erect and still to seek out the approaching enemy, and then they are fine marks for a bowman.

The stag often bores of his pasture and wishes for a change. He gathers together his companions in a great herd to seek new grasses. Coming to the bank of a river, the herd does an unusual thing. Each stag places his head on the rump of that before him, and thus they save one another from drowning as they cross the water.

In the season for mating the stag bells loudly through the forest so the females may find him. But the female can only conceive at the time of the star Arcturus. The mother hides her young cleverly in the bushes. Whenever danger threatens she stamps her foot to warn them. When they are lithe enough, the mother teaches them to run and leap in the manner of their sires.

Stag's horn, if it is burnt, is excellent for preventing snakes in one's house. The right horn is better for healing. The stag is never feverish and the marrow of a stag's bones prevents fevers in men. The flesh of the beast, called venison, is very nourishing and keeps a man free from sickness.

Reverse of lusterware dish • *Spanish (Valencia), 1435-65* • *Purchase, 1956*

Enlarged page from The Hours of Jeanne d'Évreux • *French (Paris), 1325-28*
Purchase, 1954

the UNICORN is a wondrous beast with a single long horn in the center of his forehead. With it the unicorn can wound the great elephant in his belly and thus conquer the largest of animals. He has cloven hooves and can run so fast in the forest that none can catch him. There is one ruse, however, whereby the unicorn can be trapped.

If a virgin girl is led into the woods and seated on a hillock, the unicorn will be attracted to her from afar off. He will come gladly and lay his head in her lap, embracing her and surrendering himself to her. It is then that the hunter can come with his spear and kill the unicorn.

For the unicorn's horn is a valuable prize. It absorbs the poison that the serpent spreads on the waters of the forest to kill the animals. In the evening, according to the Greek Physiologus, the unicorn goes to the stream and places his horn in the water, which is thus purified. For this reason the horn is valued among men as proof against poison.

The unicorn is likened to Christ, who also came on earth through the graces of a virgin and was betrayed by men. And in St. Luke (I:69) one reads this parallel, "He hath raised up a horn of salvation for us in the house of his son David."

The Unicorn at the Fountain · From the Unicorn Tapestries · *French or Flemish, about 1500 · Gift of John D. Rockefeller, Jr., 1937*

Doorway from the House of the Unicorns in Montferrand · *French (Auvergne), early XVI century · Purchase, 1948*

the manticore

lives far to the East in the Indies. This beast has the face of a man, but with gleaming red eyes and with three rows of teeth which meet alternately in its horrible mouth. It has the body of a lion and with its tail it can sting like a scorpion. It is difficult to escape from the manticore, which has the strength to make great leaps with its powerful legs. Its claws are as dangerous as those of the lion and it is excessively fond of human flesh. Only its voice recommends the manticore. It utters sounds like the notes of a fine flute.

Archway from St. Cosmus, Narbonne · *French (Languedoc), second half of the XII century · Kennedy Fund, 1922*

 THE BASILISK is the king of serpents. The body of this fearsome creature is patterned with white stripes as long as a hand. It lives mostly in the dry desert, like the scorpion. It has the power to kill creatures in many ways. Its very smell can wither its enemies, and to look into its eye is sure death for a man. Its hiss is so terrible that many have died from merely hearing the noise, and others have been burned up by the intense heat of its mouth before the creature even bit them. It is well known that a flying bird cannot cross the path of the basilisk unharmed, for even at a distance the bird is poisoned and falls to the ground.

Like other serpents, basilisks have an enemy in the weasel, which can conquer them unharmed. If a weasel is introduced into the basilisk's cave the king of serpents will flee, but the weasel will overtake and slay it. This shows that God made nothing without a cure.

❋

Archway from St. Cosmus, Narbonne · *French (Languedoc), second half of the XII century · Kennedy Fund, 1922*

the GRIFFIN is an animal that flies through the air. It is fearsome to see for it has the body and claws of the lion and the wings, head, and fierce beak of the eagle. All men should fear it because it feasts upon them at any opportunity. It is also extremely fond of eating horses. It is seen in these parts but rarely as it lives mostly in high mountains or in Hyperborean lands.

Capital from San Martín, Fuentidueña · *Spanish (Segovia), late XII century · Loan from the Spanish Government*

36

SIRENS, OR HARPIES

according to the Physiologus, are vicious and dangerous creatures. They are formed like human beings down to the navel, but have the wings and tail of a bird. They sing enchanting songs with their beautiful voices to lure poor sailors toward their doom. The sailors are so taken by the melody that they are soon lulled to sleep. The sirens then pounce upon them and rend them limb from limb.

The human being, walking his own ways in life, should beware of such false music that may lead to pernicious pleasures. For in being lulled and put off guard, one allows the Devil a chance to pounce on his soul.

Capital from San Martín, Fuentidueña · *Spanish (Segovia), late XII century · Loan from the Spanish Government*

the mermaid,

according to Bishop Theobald, is a name sometimes given to the siren. It is a very different creature, although with much the same history as the Harpy. The mermaid's body is fair like that of a young maiden, but where her legs should be is a long silvery fishtail. The mermaid has often been seen in the hollow of a wave combing her long hair and preening before a mirror. Her voice, too, is sweet and melodious, and as it drifts over the sea sailors may be attracted to it and turn their ship from its course. If they do, they are utterly destroyed and never are heard from again.

Capital from San Martín, Fuentidueña · *Spanish (Segovia), late XII century* · *Loan from the Spanish Government*

the ÐRAGON

breeds in lands where there is great heat, like Ethiopia and India. It is of the serpent family. When it flies through the air it gives off great heat of its own. It has a crest on its head and a narrow gullet which serves both for breathing and for sticking out its tongue. Although it is not generally believed, the dragon has no poison in its jaws or tail; it kills its victims by strangling them in its coils. It grows so large that it does not even fear the great elephant. The dragon often lies in wait where the elephant roams and trips him up by seizing his legs. As the elephant cannot rise, the dragon has an easy time coiling about him and devouring him.

Bronze aquamanile · *German, XII or XIII century · Purchase, 1947*

39

the amphisbaena

is a strange serpent with two heads. One is properly placed but the other is at the end of the tail. It is said that when one head is awake the other sleeps. Only one watches the eggs at a time. The amphisbaena can move equally well in either direction. When it comes to a hill it takes one head in the mouth of the other and rolls along like a hoop. The amphisbaena is very resistant to cold weather and is one of the earliest snakes to emerge from hibernation. Lucan wrote of the creature that it had eyes that shone like lamps.

NOTE: There are many medieval dragons depicted with two heads, like this one, which may or may not be intended to represent an amphisbaena.

Archway from St. Cosmus, Narbonne • *French (Languedoc), second half of the XII century* • *Kennedy Fund, 1922*

the CENTAUR is a lustful animal that lives deep in the forests and is seldom seen by men. Its body is formed like that of a horse, but from the belly upwards it is like a man. Centaurs combine the swiftness and sureness of foot of the horse with the heart and head of a man. They can cry for sorrow and use their intelligence to fashion weapons like a man, but they have the passions and lusts of an animal.

Saint Jerome tells us that when Saint Anthony went to visit Saint Paul in the desert, he met a centaur along the way. And though most centaurs are wild and vicious to men, this one pointed in the direction of the hermit's den to help Saint Anthony. It could not speak, of course, because from the mouths of centaurs come only the sounds of an animal.

Archway from St. Cosmus, Narbonne · *French (Languedoc), second half of the XII century · Kennedy Fund, 1922*

the salamander is a reptile with legs. It is the most poisonous of all creatures. While various serpents can kill one victim at a time, the salamander can kill many at any given moment. If it falls into a well, the water is poisoned and those who drink it will perish. If it climbs a tree, the fruits become tainted with its venom in the same fashion.

The salamander is so cold by nature that it prevails against fire. It can indeed put flames out. In the midst of a hot fire it is not burnt, and the fire soon subsides from the very nature of the serpent.

Iron doorknocker · *European, XVI century · Purchase, 1952*

snakes

flicker their tongues faster than any other beast. Thus they often seem to have three tongues. Their eyes are placed more in their foreheads than in their faces, and their eyesight is bad.

There are three facts to be noted about snakes. First, that when they grow old and blind they can renew their youth. To do this they first go to the forest and fast until their old hide has become loose. Then they find a suitable crevice in the rock and crawl through it, pulling off their old skins and shedding their old age with it. Secondly, a snake does not carry its poison with it when it goes to drink water, but first spits it out in a hole in the earth. One need not, therefore, fear a snake near the water. Thirdly, a snake lives in mortal fear of a naked man. If it spies a man wearing clothes, however, it will rush at him and strike him.

The bodies of snakes are damp and they are not equipped with feet. They crawl easily by exerting the pressure of their scales on the ends of their ribs, which are spread evenly from their throat to their belly. If a snake is struck in any part of his body, he is disabled because his back is broken.

When attacked, a snake fears for his head more than for any part of his body. He then so arranges himself in his coils that the head is at the center defended by the body itself. Also if he be cut into pieces the snake will live so long as two fingers breadth remain attached to the head.

Corbel from San Martín, Fuentidueña · *Spanish (Segovia), late XII century · Loan from the Spanish Government*

the CROW is a long-lived bird that is much used by diviners to fore-

tell the future. For the crow is fond of spying upon the doings of men, particularly in their treachery, and it stores up knowledge as it grows older. A crow often gives warning of what shall come to pass. It is not true, however, that this bird knows the secrets of God.

Crows are fine parents and store food in their nest for their young. They also accompany them in flight lest any mischance should befall them. The nature of the children is such that if the parents grow old and lose their feathers, the young crows care for them, cover them with their young feathers, and bring food to them.

The crow leaves his nesting place for a part of the year and leads the flights of storks over the seas. While in the company of the storks, they will defend them against other birds, and often when they return from their wanderings they are covered with wounds and are hoarse in their voices from their fighting.

NOTE: See page 56

Capital from San Martín, Fuentidueña · *Spanish (Segovia), late XII century · Loan from the Spanish Government*

44

the pelican

is a bird that lives near the fastness of the desert beside the Nile River. All the food that the pelican eats it cleanses in the water. When its meal is washed, this strange bird places the food in its mouth with its foot, as if it were a hand.

The pelican loves her children too much. When they grow large in the nest they flap their wings in the faces of their parents and peck at them. In pecking back the mother kills her children. For three days she mourns them. Then, with her beak she opens her own breast so that her life blood can flow over the infants. This restores them to life.

The sacrifice of the pelican is similar to that of Christ, who created mankind in his own image and witnessed mankind's evil ways. For this reason he ascended to the cross, where his side was pierced, and the blood and water that flowed from it was for the salvation of mankind.

Archway from St. Cosmus, Narbonne • *French (Languedoc), second half of the XII century • Kennedy Fund, 1922*

45

the partRidge is a cunning bird with many bad habits. One

hen often steals eggs from another's nest and hatches them as her own. It does her
no good at all, as it turns out, for the chicks recognize their own mother and immediately return to the proper nest.

Partridges have coats which blend with the foliage. However, if they think they
have been seen, they turn over on their backs and cover themselves with dirt so
as to be completely hidden. They cover their eggs also with dust to hide them and
they build their nests in thorny places so that marauders are kept at bay. As the
father birds often attack the young, the hens must guard against them also.

Whenever a man approaches the nesting place of a partridge, the mother shows
herself on purpose and feigns lameness or a broken wing, wandering off slowly,
away from the nest. She may coax the intruder a long distance before giving up her
ruse. Then she disappears into the brush. Thus she shows great cleverness in pro-
tecting her family.

Partridges are very lascivious birds. It is said that if the female stands upwind
from the male she may become pregnant.

Detail from the Unicorn Tapestries · *French or Flemish, about 1500* · *Gift of John D.*
Rockefeller, Jr., 1937

46

THE MAGPIE is a remarkable bird that can imitate the voice of a man with great precision. It cannot carry on a real conversation, of course, but when magpies sit in the trees and chatter one would think that they were talking together. It was Martial who wrote, "I, a magpie and a talker, greet thee, Lord, with clear speech, and if you did not see me, you would refuse to believe that I am a bird."

Detail from the Campin Altarpiece • *Flemish (Tournai), about 1425* • *Purchase*

fĺṡḣ live all their lives in the water. Like the flocks of sheep and herds of cattle of the land, they join together in large groups, called schools. They have the proper shape and nature for swimming. Though they may not be fast in the water, yet they can plunge into the greatest depths of the ocean.

the whale is the greatest fish of the sea. It was such a fish that swallowed Jonah. The whale is wont to lie in the sunshine on the top of the sea, so that often a garden of grass and bushes grows upon his back. Sailors seeing this think that they have found land. They tie up their ship beside the whale and climb upon him and build a fire. When the whale feels the heat of the fire on his back he plunges into the ocean, taking the sailors and their ship to their doom.

When the whale desires to eat, he exhales a sweet breath with the odor of flowers. Then all the little fish rush toward the sweet smell. They crowd together into the whale's mouth and he devours them. But he eats little fish only; he cannot feed on big ones.

Detail of a lusterware dish • *Spanish (Valencia), 1420-30 • Purchase, 1956*

48

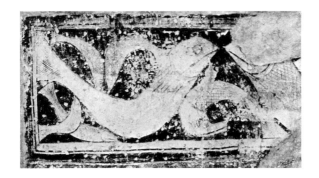

ÐOLPHINS are known to follow the sound of the human voice, or even to gather together at the sound of music. There is no fish in the sea that is swifter than they, nor any that enjoy more to play in the surf and the waves. Often they follow ships, which they could easily overtake and pass. A dolphin can tell by the smell of a dead man if he had ever eaten a dolphin's flesh. If he had not, the dolphins push his body to the shore, but if he had, they devour him on the spot.

the CRAB is a fish that lives in a shell and has legs. It lives both in rivers and in the sea. Crabs are the mortal enemies of oysters on which they enjoy feasting. Because the oyster is so well provided with a strong shell, which the crab can neither break nor open, the crab resorts to a trick to obtain his dinner. When the innocent oyster lies relaxing with its shell open, the crab tosses in a stone so the shell cannot close. Then can the crab feast merrily on the soft meat of the oyster.

Fresco from San Pedro de Arlanza · *Spanish, about 1220* · *Purchase, 1931*

Enlarged detail from The Hours of Jeanne d'Évreux · *French (Paris), 1325-28* · *Purchase, 1954*

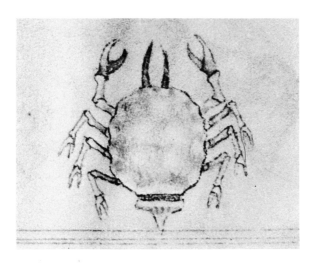

the peacock

the peacock is a magnificent bird with wings and tail feathers that are as bright as if they were jeweled. His flesh is harder than that of any other creature and therefore it does not putrefy. It is also not readily cooked.

Because his body is so beautiful the peacock is self-conscious of his feet. Whenever he glances down and sees his awkward black feet, he screams aloud in horror. His voice is raucous and unpleasant, but it is said that the cries of the peacock foretell the weather.

Detail of a stained-glass panel · *German, 1518* · *Purchase, 1930*

the hawk is a bird with a small body but of great courage. It is very swift in flight and is noted for the rapaciousness with which it seizes its prey in its talons. It is often called a thief and a ravisher.

The hawk trains its children to become capable thieves in the following way: when they are old enough to leave the nest or to try their wings, it brings them no food, but beats them with its wings and forces them out into the world. The hawk does not wish them to be spoiled and to grow up worthless, for it dreads inactivity and debauchery. The young hawks must therefore grow strong and seek their own prey. Thus at a tender age they become skilled in the art of stealing.

Detail of a lusterware dish · *Spanish (Valencia), 1420-30 · Purchase, 1956*

the crane

is a bird with great, strong wings that flies high in the air so that he may see his destination from far off. He enjoys the company of his fellows and flies together with them in a regular formation. One crane is the pathfinder and leads the formation, calling out to the others and chastising those that lag behind. If this one should get hoarse, another takes his place. When cranes flying thus get tired, their stronger fellows support them with their wings until they are rested.

They are very adept at keeping guard by night, and they set regular sentries who relieve one another. In order to avoid falling asleep, each sentry crane stands on one foot and holds a stone in the other. In case he should become drowsy and drop the stone, he will immediately awake and return to his duty. If any danger threatens, the sentry calls out in a loud voice and wakes his fellows.

One might think from their fragile appearance that a high wind would blow a crane from his path. In order to prevent this they eat a ballast of stones and thus have enough weight to maintain their course. When a crane grows old he turns black.

NOTE: The illustration depicts a heron, which is not mentioned in the bestiary.

Reverse of lusterware dish • *Spanish (Valencia), 1435-65* • *Purchase, 1956*

the DOVE nests in the crevice of a rock. It is a bird of great love, as one can see from its eye, and often brings up the young of other birds that have been abandoned. In old age it knows how to recover its lost sight. The dove enjoys the company of others and so travels in great flocks. Doves defend themselves with their wings. Or, more cleverly, to avoid the hawk they sit on branches near a stream. If they see the shadow of a hawk, they dive quickly into the water and thus escape. The song of the dove is poor and sounds more like a croak than a birdsong.

Its cousin the turtle-dove has one noteworthy characteristic. It takes only one mate in its life. If this one is killed, it feels cheated and spurns love and will never mate again.

❋

Enameled ciborium · *French (Limoges), XIII century · Purchase, 1947*

the DUCK

spends almost his whole life in swimming. There are many varieties of ducks, some of which feed more than others on marsh grass. Like all other birds they have the peculiarity of being born twice. The duck is born once when the egg is laid and again by the heat of his mother's body when the egg is hatched.

the GOOSE

is the cousin of the duck and also spends much time in the water, swimming from one spot to another. Geese divide the night into watches and they mark the changing of the watch with a great deal of cackling. They are wise in noting the approach of men from their scent. It was geese who first apprised the Romans that the Gauls were clambering over the walls of Rome.

Capital from Bonnefont-en-Comminges · *French (Gascony), first half of the XIV century · Purchase, 1925*

Enlarged detail from The Hours of Jeanne d'Évreux · *French (Paris), 1325-28 Purchase, 1954*

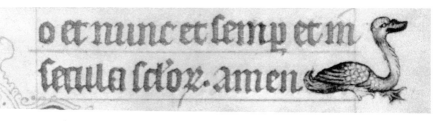

54

the swan is a bird of beautiful voice, for it has a long neck to make rich and varied notes. In Hyperborean lands, it is said, when the harpers come to play in the castles, the swans fly out of their nests to join in the concert, always singing in strict measure.

The ancients found the swan most good in auguries and sailors think of it as a sign against shipwreck. This latter idea comes from the fact that the swan spurns to plunge itself beneath the water.

When swans wish to make love they twine their necks together.

❋

Detail from the Unicorn Tapestries · *French or Flemish, about 1500* · *Gift of John D. Rockefeller, Jr., 1937*

the owl
thrives on darkness and flies about in the night. It sees nothing in the sunlight. In the day it acts as though it were blind.

The crow is the owl's enemy. When a crow finds an owl during the day, he calls his companions who join together to mob the owl.

The owl is a symbol of darkness and hence of the Jews who rejected Christ, the light of the world, as their king; for they said, "We have no King but Caesar."

NOTE: The owl's head carved on the capital here illustrated has been partially damaged. Two crows are shown attacking their enemy.   See page 44

Capital from San Martín, Fuentidueña · *Spanish (Segovia), late XII century · Loan from the Spanish Government*

the eagle is noted for its wonderful eyes which can see at a great distance. When it flies so high in the air that the eye of man cannot discern it, the eagle can see the small fishes in the sea and will dive down and capture them in its claws.

When an eagle reaches old age, its eyes begin to dim and its feathers to wilt. It then seeks out a fair fountain in the forest and from this it flies aloft and straight into the sun. When its feathers are singed and its eyes burned from approaching the sun, the eagle dives into the cool fountain and there its eyes are washed clean, its feathers restored, and its youth regained.

In a somewhat similar fashion the eagle tests the worth of its own young. When they are still unable to fly, it lifts them up and flies toward the sun. Those that can look straight into the sun are deemed worthy and are returned to the nest, while those whose eyes water or who look away are thought to be worthless and are cast down.

Carved wood lectern · *French or Flemish, XV century · Purchase, 1925*

the COCK

the COCK is the timekeeper of the world. His crowing is not only a pleasant thing to hear, but it serves many good purposes. It wakes those who are sleeping, even the animals of the barnyard, and its clear notes carry far in the morning air. By this herald of the morning the traveler notes the passage of time, the sailor is assured that the storm will abate at daybreak, the thief knows to leave his business, and the priest recognizes the hour for prayer. Even the morning star complies with the crow of the cock and shines in the heavens.

The meat of the cock is said to be excellent medicine if eaten with a mixture of liquid gold.

Enlarged detail from The Hours of Jeanne d'Évreux • *French (Paris), 1325-28*
Purchase, 1954

the STORK

has no tongue to speak with but makes a clacking sound with its beak by shaking its head. Storks are considered the messengers of spring, as they migrate across far lands and waters. They always fly in formation, sometimes as far as to Asia. Crows accompany them as pathfinders on their long flights.

The stork is a fine mother who cares long and lovingly for her babies. She stays with them so long at the nest that she loses her feathers. Then the babies return her favors by caring for her until she regains her plumage.

Detail from a lusterware dish · *Spanish (Valencia), second half of the XV century*
Purchase, 1956

index